- Marina Carlos -

I'll figure it out:

How ableism impacts disabled people's lives

Illustrated by Freaks

ISBN - Ebook: 978-2-9572268-2-5.
ISBN - Paperback: 978-2-9572268-1-8.
Legal deposit: 2020.
Printed in 2020 by Marina Carlos as a self-published author. Illustrations and design by Freaks.
Fonts used: Franklin Gothic Book, DK brush Crush, DK coal Brush, Cardieno Modern, Sepet, Simplicity.

AUTHOR'S NOTE

I wrote this book with the outlook of a person with reduced mobility, as my personal experience is one of a wheelchair user. Therefore, the numerous examples which I focused on are the obstacles I face daily.

Nevertheless, it's important to remember that a motor disability is just one type of disability among others and that invisible disabilities also exist.

TABLE OF CONTENTS

"ABLEISM IS TRASH!"

- Mia Mingus & Amita Swadhin -

ABLEISM

Ableism refers to the systemic oppression of disabled people, from prejudice to discrimination. It's a term that has been used for years by researchers, activists and institutions such as the United Nations and which causes disability to be seen as 'other' and a condition to overcome. For example, contrary to able-bodied people, disabled people:

- can be seen as charity cases,
- can be mocked,
- can't easily access public spaces,
- can be seen as asexual and non-desirable,
- are not represented in media.

The social norm identifies an able-bodied person as 'standard' or 'normal', which therefore characterizes a disabled person as 'non-standard', 'abnormal' and even inferior. Because of that, disabled people are not treated the same way, are marginalized and their needs aren't taken into account.

Despite laws and international conventions that support the rights of disabled people to have equal rights to other people, the general lack of respect towards disabled people - which is socially accepted - is why they aren't put into practice. Because of this, disabled people have enormous difficulties in accessing education, employment, housing, leisure activities, healthcare etc.

Concretely, people with disabilities exist in the same timeline as able-bodied people yet spend their time adjusting to live their lives.

Thus, the 'I'll figure it out' becomes a way of life for them.

Having to ask for help because the lack of access prevents them from being autonomous.

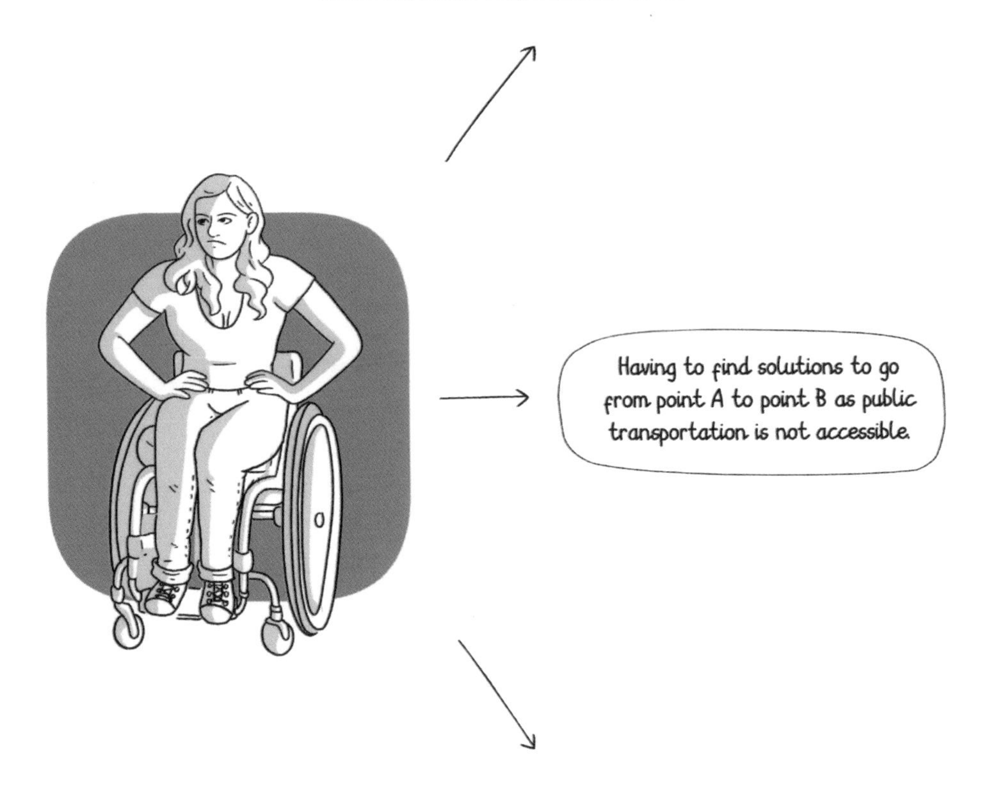

Having to work isolated from home or in a particular space because the company's offices are not accessible.

Ableism creates substantial costs for disabled people. They have additional expenses to cover because of their disabilities that welfare and social assistance don't cover, even though people with disabilities are already living precariously.

In the United Kingdom, this is called 'the disability price tag' (1) - or 'disability tax' in the United States. In 2019, the report of the British organization Scope indicates that in the UK:

• disabled adults spend on average £583 - or $751 - more than able-bodied adults a month for the costs linked to their disability.

• on average, a disabled adult's extra costs are equivalent to almost half of their income (after housing costs).

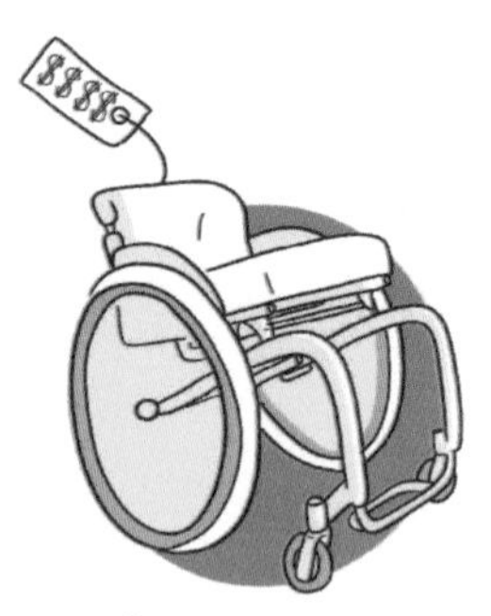

Ableism is also present in interactions between able-bodied and disabled people, where the latter are often ignored or infantilized. As well, during a time when 'consent' is highly discussed following the #MeToo movement, it's important to remember that disabled people also need to offer consent concerning their bodies and equipment (e.g. wheelchair, cane, etc.). Touching, pushing, or grabbing someone and their equipment, which is considered an extension of their body, without them being consulted and/or without their consent is a violation of their bodies.

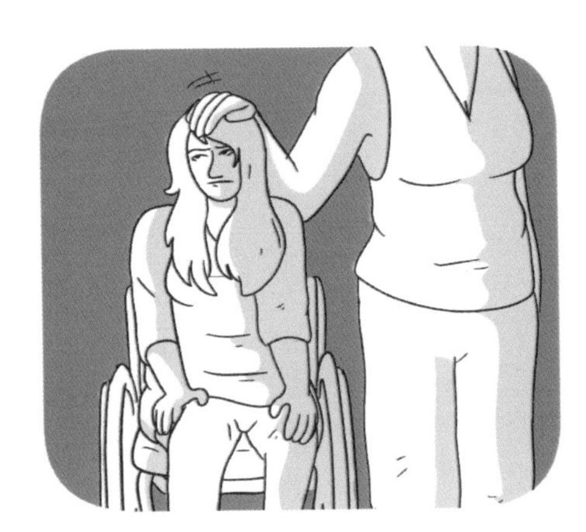

As D'Arcee Neal, a black gay disabled American advocate, writes: 'The truth is that for most disabled people, consent factors into our daily lives in ways that it doesn't for the able-bodied. [...] The experiences of the disabled teach that it actually serves as a mutual platform of respect, regardless of situation and circumstances (2).'

In 2017, queer Korean activist Mia Mingus wrote a text about those interactions and particularly regarding what she calls:

FORCED INTIMACY

This term 'refers to the common daily experience of disabled people being expected to share personal parts of ourselves to survive in an ableist world (3)'. For example, forced intimacy happens when:

- a disabled person is being asked intimate questions.

- a disabled person's wheelchair is pushed by someone they don't know (to board a plane for example).

In those kinds of moments, that consent is often given under pressure as disabled people don't have any other choice to access a location or service, and as a result, have to depend on this other person, even if they don't necessarily trust them. Therefore, they find themselves in a vulnerable position.

In these situations, since disabled people are treated as children, they often find themselves facing service providers and staff who think they know the persons' body and disability better than the person knows themselves.

CASUAL ABLEISM

Casual ableism describes every barrier and comment that disabled people are subjected to daily and that keep them marginalized and considered as 'other'.

Some remarks are claimed to be compliments, such as:

The problem with this sort of compliments is that what they imply is: 'You're disabled so why would you want to do things?'. So, even if those comments claim to be empathetic, in reality, they illustrate the ableist idea that disability is intrinsically dreadful, something negative and that it's impossible to want to live or keep living while having a disability.

Subsequently, ableism sidesteps interactions between able-bodied and disabled people. Indeed, their presence in a space quickly makes other people uncomfortable. This 'awkwardness' is particularly highlighted when able-bodied people ask 'how they should talk to disabled people'even though there is no 'user manual' as disabled people are just... well... people.

Although there isn't a particular language to speak to people with disabilities, the discomfort is so real that some behavior patterns from able-bodied people exist in friendships, relationships, at work etc.

- Asking intrusive questions,
- questioning their disability,
- not considering their needs and/or boundaries,
- making them feel guilty for being disabled and/or dependant,
- thinking they know the disability better than the disabled person themselves,
- helping a person with disabilities then asking for endless gratitude.

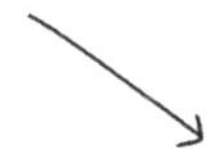

In short, the lesson is that it is important to show respect as a bare minimum in any relationship. Disability or not.

Those words and behaviors illustrate what the majority of disabled people fear and put up with. And since little is being done to allow them to be as autonomous as possible, they find themselves being quickly dependant on others. Consequently, words like 'burden' are often used to describe them and they can feel guilty and become self-conscious about having to ask for help.

The guilt, the sense of not being enough or that their needs are too complicated to handle are common feelings caused by ableism. These ideas are so persistent that they not only impact relationships, but also disabled people's own perception of themselves within those relationships. These ideas are so pervasive that they often become internalized by people with disabilities.

INTERNALIZED ABLEISM

... consists in having, as a disabled person, an ableist outlook on society, where people with disabilities are less worthy than able-bodied people. In concrete terms, this can lead disabled people to 'bite the bullet' and attempt to 'normalize' themselves whatever the cost to be accepted.

For disabled people, internalized ableism is a really difficult thing to perceive and deconstruct as ableism is everywhere all the time. As a result, numerous people with disabilities see themselves as burdens, tend to make self-deprecating jokes to try to be accepted and think they are too demanding if they want the minimum (the minimum being the same thing as an able-bodied person).

MEDICAL AND SOCIAL MODELS OF DISABILITY

For several years, some institutions like the United Nations, researchers and disabled activists have been advocating to redefine the notion of disability.

They want to move away from the prominent medical model which engenders a view of society where disability is a problem that must be 'fixed', and move towards the social model, which is centered around the organization of society and the need to dismantle structural barriers thus allowing disabled people to be fully included as they are.

However, demanding that disabled people's rights be respected doesn't mean that a disability or chronic illness in itself cannot have serious and direct consequences on someone's body and life. As @twitchyspoonie explains on Twitter:

TheDisabilityEnthusiast @twitchyspoonie

Sometimes accommodations won't "fix" everything. It's ok if the social model doesn't totally fit your experience. It's ok if you want treatment/a cure. It's ok if you don't like your disabilities all the time. The only important thing banding us all together is that we want our human rights [...]. (4)

People with disabilities deserve the same human rights and autonomy as able-bodied people. Therefore, ableism is an oppression to tackle with the aim towards the respect of disabled people, so that they can live their lives as autonomously as possible.

"ACCESS IS LOVE."

- Alice Wong, Mia Mingus & Sandy Ho -

ACCESSIBILITY

Accessibility is one of the main priorities when it comes to the rights of disabled people, as it represents one of the major obstacles of their daily lives.

Lack of accessibility is prevalent in all areas of life, including housing, employment, transportation, education, healthcare, and more. When it's physically impossible for disabled people to navigate on sidewalks, enter a building, take public transportation, go out to have a drink or go to a concert, disabled people's segregation is a fact.

Therefore, they are excluded from public and private spaces and prevented from being autonomous.

PUBLIC TRANSPORTATION

In September 2017, The Guardian (1) published an article comparing subway accessibility in several cities around the World. Compared with Los Angeles, Tokyo or Barcelona, Paris is largely behind with a huge lack of accessible stations.

Only 9 of the 303 Parisian subway stations are accessible - when elevators are working - and every one of them is located on the line 14, opened in 1998.

Parisian subway map

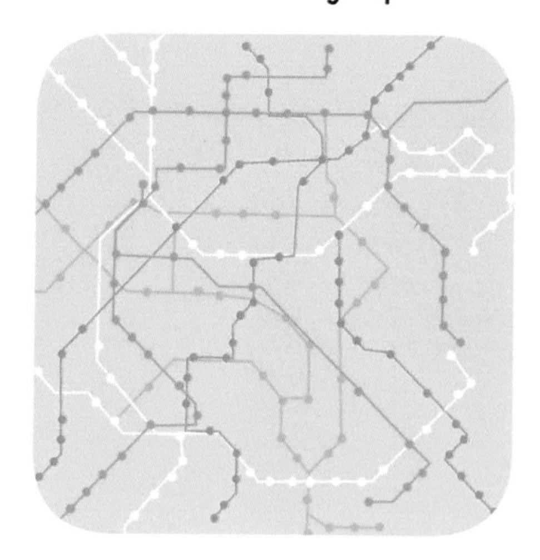

Accessible Parisian subway map

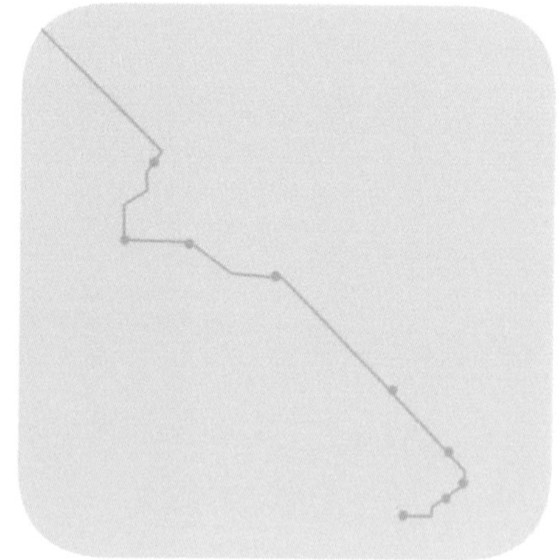

This situation highlights the difficulties that disabled people face to navigate freely in and around Paris. It's upsetting listening to politicians as they advocate for accessibility construction to be accelerated for the 2024 Paris Summer Olympics and Paralympics. As if the argument that the city isn't accessible to disabled Parisians wasn't persuasive enough.

Priorities...

DISABLED PEOPLE:

We would like to access the subway in Paris.

PARIS:

We're going to give our subways a blue makeover! [2]

These decisions prevent disabled citizens from being able to enjoy the same rights as other citizens, especially those regarding autonomy and mobility.

As far as other types of public transportation are concerned, there's the bus. On paper, the majority of buses are accessible within the French city, but in actuality, it's a different story.

Accessibility has to be taken into account in all areas, including the surroundings of bus stops, the working order of the bus, the training of drivers, and the conscientiousness of passengers. For example, even if the International Symbol of Access (the wheelchair symbol) is displayed on the bus demonstrating it is accessible, other factors prevent the situation from being accessible, such as when:

- the driver ignores you,
- the driver doesn't stop the bus correctly,
- the ramp isn't working,
- the other passengers don't move to give you space to enter and place yourself safely.

The tramway is one of the most accessible transportation means but it only exists in the capital's outskirts. Furthermore, the services offered by the Parisian City Hall, the PAM (transportation for people with disabilities), isn't a reliable and effective service.

In short, disabled people's mobility options in Paris are very limited.

These types of barriers are not unique to Paris, and in fact exist all across France and all over the world, thus reflecting a common difficulty disabled people encounter when navigating public spaces.

> New York City buses are wheelchair accessible but disabled riders still face obstacles.

citylimits.org (3)

> Why London's subway system leaves so many disabled people without a ride.

cbc.ca (4)

In these circumstances, taxis - of which some expenses can be funded by the State after completing administrative procedures - or a personal vehicle can be alternatives. Nonetheless, making adjustments to a car is a considerable cost and disabled people's parking spaces aren't always available. Therefore, a dilemma appears: taxi or car?

- The benefits of taking a cab include not having to think about where to park and using less energy. But, as taxis are rarely accessible, asking for help from the driver becomes necessary (hello forced intimacy) and thus, autonomy is impacted.

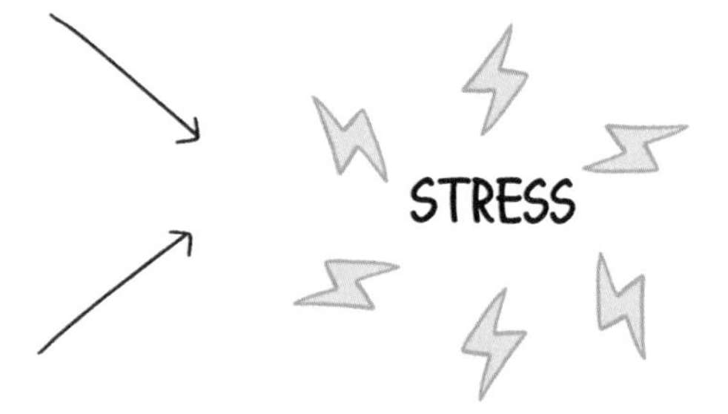

- Having a car allows more independence but then, multiple questions come up: Is there going to be an accessible parking space? How far is the parking space from the location? Is the path from the parking space to the location easy to navigate?

To continue the discussion of parking spaces reserved for disabled people and holders of the Carte Mobilité Inclusion (CMI, the French disabled parking permit): you can find them here and there on public roads or parking lots. They are larger than the 'regular' parking spaces and are supposed to allow disabled drivers to enter and exit their vehicle safely.

The card is allocated under certain conditions and must be appended visibly on the windshield.

Yet, there is negligence: numerous parking spaces are situated on the left side of the road, which means that they are, in the end, inaccessible for some disabled people.

How so, you may ask? Because if the person parks in a parking space located on the left side of the road, as a driver, they will now be near the sidewalk.

When the driver will open the door, they will be able to put the wheelchair on the sidewalk but they will not necessarily be able to carry out the transfer from the driver's seat to the wheelchair because the latter will be too high compared to the driver's seat as the sidewalk will be higher than the road.

Driver's parking space on the right side of the road.

There is practically no gap between the transfer tablet* and the wheelchair.

Driver's parking space on the left side of the road.

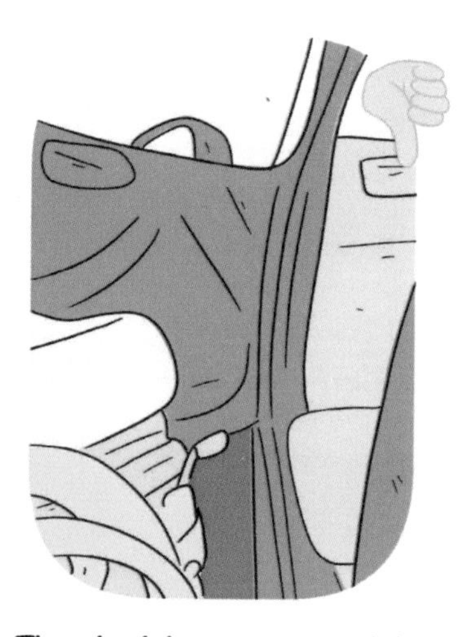

The wheelchair is now much higher than the transfer tablet and makes the transfer too dangerous.

Consequently, a lot of drivers with a disability can only park on reserved parkings spaces on the right side of the road or find 'regular' parking spaces even though the first ones are supposed to be made for them also.

* A transfer tablet helps to reduce the distance between the driver's seat and the wheelchair.

CONCERTS

In big concert venues, the area for people with reduced mobility are located at the top of the venue... where their sight will be blocked by spectators who, obviously, will get up during a live show.

As a matter of fact, Paris' Zénith wrote on its website (5), in black and white, that 'bleacher seats for people with disabilities have a good stage visibility as long as audience members in the bleachers don't stand up'. They don't see any problem making disabled spectators pay to see nothing. Bold move.

Smaller venues don't have specific areas for disabled people, which makes it hard to find a place to really enjoy the concert.

All in all, most of the time, it's really simple: disabled people pay to see nothing or very little and are not seated near their friends, family or significant others, whom are often seated in front or behind them. Moreover, these venues generally place people with reduced mobility together, separated from able-bodied people... just like it happens in society.

TRAVEL

Traveling while disabled turns out to be frequently laborious because despite all the anticipation and organization, the trip can actually not go as smoothly as planned and this can start from the airport...

- where the staff don't really know how to assist a disabled person (who is often called 'the wheelchair' if they use one),

- when various airlines, airports and service providers don't communicate between themselves the disabled passenger's needs,

- when equipment, such as wheelchairs, are broken or lost because of bad management even though that equipment is expensive and essential for disabled people's autonomy.

In the United States, airlines break or lose 26 wheelchairs on average per day. (6)

... to the accommodation:

Efforts are made regarding hotels but also in services like Airbnb or Booking.com, where filters are now available, but there's a lot more that has to be done to allow disabled travelers to travel as comfortably and serenely as their able-bodied counterparts.

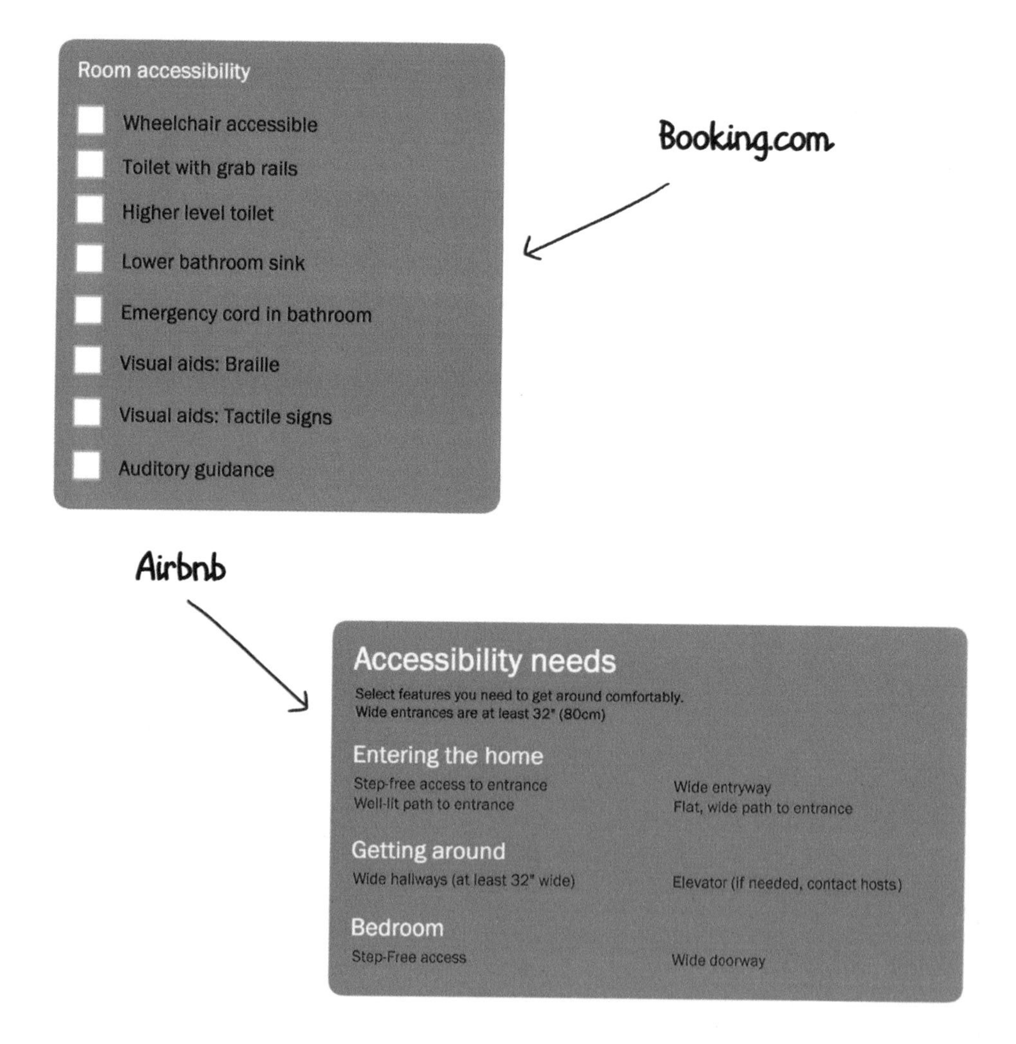

Often, 'social spaces' (coffee shops, restaurants, clubs...) point out that they don't find it essential to make adjustments because they have little to none disabled clientele, completely omitting the fact that disabled people aren't not coming because they don't exist but because they can't access it.

Gabrielle Peters @mssinenomine

Pro-tip: A really good way to make sure you keep things as inaccessible as possible is to design them to be inaccessible and then decide you don't have money to make them accessible. (7)

As a matter of fact, these places tend to also be the ones that will say 'Yes, it's accessible! There is just a little step!' whereas that 'little step' is the obstacle that will prevent disabled people to enter these establishments.

This highlights the fact that able-bodied people don't have the same definition of accessibility than disabled people, which is supposed to take into account full autonomy. Also, they don't see the necessity to include people with disabilities - who know about these things because they experience it daily - from the conception or beginning of the renovation of a place.

These experiences regarding facing lack of accessibility are not anecdotes to try to fix one-by-one but reflect a larger problem: disabled people don't have the same rights to live and navigate spaces as able-bodied people.

And when the simple fact of going out has to be thoroughly planned and that, despite all the energy already spent, it can end up becoming an umpteenth negative or discriminatory experience, this can lead disabled people to isolate themselves even further. This type of 'preparation' created by an ableist society is what I call:

CONSTRUCTED ANXIETY

When society imposes barriers everywhere, a disabled person's everyday life cannot be 'peaceful'. Spontaneity becomes almost impossible and even forbidden because it's not necessarily the person's disability that prevents them from going out, working, traveling etc, but the structural obstacles which punctuate their daily lives. And when:

- every outing has to be organized in detail,
- locations that are supposed to be accessible aren't,
- financial and human resources are not sufficient to lead an autonomous life,
- sustained looks and/or inappropriate comments occur when a disabled person exists in a space...

... It's extremely difficult and sometimes even impossible to not feel anxiety; an anxiety that could be reduced to a great extent by a society that respects and takes into account disabled people's rights.

It's important to be aware that accessibility isn't just some tangible and material adjustments like ramps or elevators but the demonstration of who can access what.

As disabled sociologist Pierre Dufour expresses: 'Choices made by the State contribute largely to determine which spaces will or won't be accessible to everyone. [...] It's a ban that doesn't really say its name but it is, indeed, one. [...] It's a choice of society, a really clear one, a choice centered around able-bodied people, a retrograde choice (8).'

Accessibility isn't an 'effort' or a 'gesture' towards disabled people but a necessary step intended for correcting discriminatory and unfair policies with the objective of establishing a just society.

"REPRESENTATION MATTERS."

MEDIA REPRESENTATION

Media plays a major role regarding representation of disabled people and continues to engage with clichés and prejudice. By reading and watching a great number of content about people with disabilities, we quickly figure out that the form and substance are almost always the same archetypes.

The way journalists talk and write about disabled people is often very reductive. The same language elements come back often and the most used format is the one of the ‘testimony‘. However, this format is problematic because it individualizes experiences of disabled people, systematically preventing the contextualization of those experiences and, thus, concealing a global oppression.

At 16, she dances despite her disability

Brut - youtube.com (1)

Warning! Huge news!

RJ Mitte, Breaking Bad actor, becomes a model despite his disability

people.bfmtv.com (2)

RJ Mitte acts in one of the biggest TV shows of the decade but apparently it's incredible for him to become a model? Okay...

Marseille: when passion overcomes disability

laprovence.com (3)

Disabled people don't "overcome" disability, they deal with it.

These headlines, which focus only on the person's disability, continue to give the impression that it's implausible to dance, become a model or be passionate about something when you're disabled... Whereas nothing happens despite disability but despite ableism.

Likewise, most journalists, who don't really know much about disability nor ableism, have a tendency to think that disabled people who, admittedly, observe, analyze behaviors and think about solutions given their experiences, just have all the knowledge and all the answers regarding this really dense subject.

> What is done nowadays to make a wheelchair user's home accessible? And why is it so expensive... we see that builders do so grudgingly? Why is that a problem? What do we do to solve this? We got the impression that nothing is done regarding disabled people? Are there any policy norms today for builders?

→ Examples of questions sent via Direct Message on Twitter by a jounalist: questions that should rather be asked to builders and politicians than to the people who are subjected to those decisions.

Certainly, disabled people are not the ones making the decision to be marginalized but able-bodied people, putting in place ableist policies, who exclude them deliberately.

In addition, a lot of articles are written about the taboo regarding disabled people's sexual lives. A subject so taboo that it has been talked about for ages: not a lot of people with disabilities haven't been asked questions such as: 'But like, how do you do it?'.

Direct Message received on Twitter from a journalist, even though I never talk about my sexual life on Social Media.

Why do a thorough research paper when you can just ask a disabled person to write an 'open letter'? →

Breaking news: there isn't 'one' sexual life of disabled people as there isn't 'one' able-bodied people's sexual life. →

Hello Marina, I'm a journalist working on a piece about sex and disability. I would like to do that in the form of a testimony, like an open letter, as a personal story is often more impactful than a long enquiry to explain the realities of disabled people's sexual lives and to break the clichés regarding that topic.

Finally, the ignorance regarding ableism and the lack of disabled people in editorial boards make it so that content stays, even today, hollow and limited to disabled people's experiences, whereas those experiences happen in a particular societal context, an ableist one.

EXAMPLES TO FOLLOW

The cost of being disabled

Imani Barbarin for designsponge.com (4)

Cutting disability services doesn't save money.
But it does damage lives

Frances Ryan for theguardian.com (5)

Selma Blair became a disabled icon overnight.
Here's why we need more stories like hers

Zipporah Arielle for bustle.com (6)

Here are some content created by disabled people (journalists or not). The themes are tangible and important: politics, representation, structural violence... However, disabled people aren't here just to produce content about disability and/or ableism!

TELEVISION

Disabled people's representation on French television is rare:

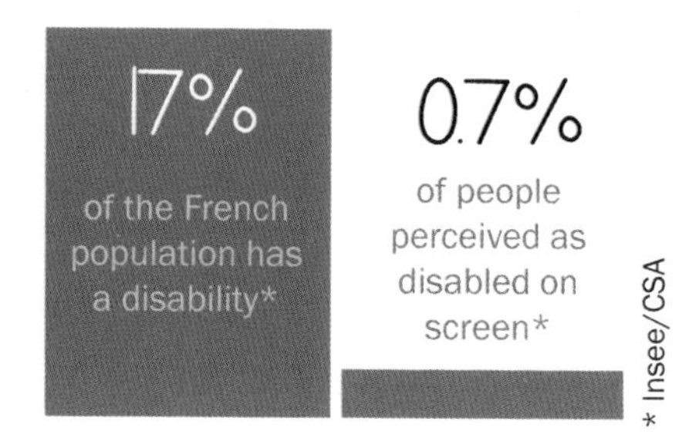

and continues to fuel clichés and prejudice by highlighting 2 extremes:

Whereas between the 2, there are a multitude of disabilities, visible and invisible, and types of disabled people that can be represented on TV.

INSPIRATION PORN

When we talk about ableist language, we often take for example 'inspiration porn', a term coined by Stella Young, an Australian comedian, journalist and advocate for disabled people's rights.

'Inspiration porn' refers to content (picture, video...) where a disabled person exists exclusively to inspire able-bodied people, motivate and make them put things into perspective:

These pictures cause a few issues:

- disabled people are objectified,
- a disability can actually limit a person,
- messages like 'the only disability in life is a bad attitude' turn the attention away from the actual problem because, as Stella Young once said:

MOVIES

These last few years, we hear a lot about diversity and authenticity in movies but disability is often forgotten:

• In 2017, 18.7% of the American population was disabled but only 2.5% of characters had a disability in the 100 most popular movies in the US (8).

• The majority of disabled characters are played by able-bodied people, which is called 'cripping up'.

These actors are all able-bodied.

... And the consequences of such practices:

• prevent disabled people to tell their stories and perpetuate a system of exclusion in front and behind the camera,

• movies are produced, written and directed by people who have an ableist perception of disability and tend to use too often the two extremes we saw previously,

• realistic and nuanced representations of disabled people are not taken to the screens,

• disabled actors are reduced to play the 'disabled person' role even though they can play the part of the son, the wife, the colleague, the friend, the partner, etc.

EXAMPLE TO FOLLOW

In the movie 'A Quiet Place' which came out in 2018, Regan, a deaf teenager, communicates in sign language with her family in order to survive creatures ultra sensitive to sound within a post- apocalyptic world... and that's all.

There is no focus on her disability, it is not perceived as something negative... In short, Regan - played by the deaf actress Millicent Simmonds - is just a badass!!

TV SHOWS

In TV shows, we notice the same inequalities. In 2016, 95% of disabled characters in the top 10 TV shows were played by able-bodied people (9). Nonetheless, these past years, several TV shows showcased disabled characters played by disabled actors.

Dustin Henderson / Gaten Matarazzo

Walter White Jr / RJ Mitte

Joey Lucas / Marlee Matlin

Furthermore, their storylines don't revolve around their disabilities but don't hide it either: Joey Lucas, who is deaf, has an interpreter when she exchanges in 'The West Wing' and 'Breaking Bad' highlights the enormous costs of treatment regarding cerebral palsy, Walter White Junior's disability.

As for Dustin, the actor has cleidocranial dysplasia. The character wasn't supposed to be disabled but the 'Stranger Things' creators then decided to include it in the story.

And soon will come out the American series 'Sanctuary', with Maysoon Zayid, about a Wall Street lawyer. It'll become the first TV show with a visibly disabled woman as the main character. As the actress explains: 'This has never been done before. We are not making history, we are changing the story (10).'

'Special' is a Netflix show that came out in 2019, which tells the daily life of Ryan, a disabled young gay man. Its topics are universal and revolve around work, dating, friendships and self-acceptance. The show got itself talked about as Ryan O'Connell, who is also disabled, wrote, played and directed it, a practice still rare nowadays.

Simultaneously, the TV show 'Titans' casted deaf genderqueer Chinese-American artist Chella Man to play the role of Joseph Wilson, aka Jericho. The father of the character did not succeed in saving him from assassins who cut his vocal cords. He became non-verbal and thus communicates in sign language, a language also used by Chella Man.

After noting the lack of authenticity and diversity regarding disabled people's representation in TV shows/movies, and inspired by the Bechdel-Wallace (11) and Kent (12) Tests, I created:

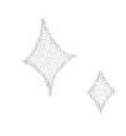

THE DISREP TEST

(for DISability REPresentation)

This test allows us to point out the diversity of people with disabilities' representation in movies and TV shows. It analyzes content along the following lines:

a) at least one disable character,
b) who isn't a cis, white, straight man,
c) who is portrayed by a disabled person,
d) whose storyline doesn't revolve around their disability (the character isn't there for miserabilism nor inspiration porn purposes),
e) who doesn't have to endure mocking nor use self-deprecating humor to be accepted (unless it's part of the character's development).

Good luck finding lots of them, not counting those mentioned previously obviously!

FASHION

Fashion seems to be going with the flow, even if there's still so much to do. We notice a higher presence of disabled models, notably in the United States and the United Kingdom, in advertising campaigns, fashion magazines and online retailers' websites.

Jillian Mercado, revealed by the Diesel Spring-Summer 2014 campaign, is a disabled Latina model and an activist who uses a wheelchair because of muscular dystrophy.

A few months after tweeting that she will take over the Fashion World, Aaron Philip became the first disabled black trans model to be signed to the renown agency Elite.

In May 2019, during the Met Gala, Sinéad Burke, an Irish educator and advocate, became the first little person to take part in the event. And a few months after, she became the first little person to be in the cover of Vogue UK, for its September issue - the most important of the year - next to Jane Fonda, Laverne Cox and Jameela Jamil, among others.

'It's essential that fashion continues to improve its diversity drive. Fashion is perhaps the only industry that we each have a tangible connection to: we all wear clothes, they touch our skin and it is a legal requirement that we get dressed every day. Whether we invest in high fashion or the high-street, we each have a perspective and a desire to feel represented (13).'

In France, it's still... THE VOID.

“THE MARGINALIZED DID NOT CREATE IDENTITY POLITICS. THEIR IDENTITIES HAVE BEEN FORCED ON THEM BY DOMINANT GROUPS AND POLITICS IS THE MOST EFFECTIVE METHOD OF REVOLT.”

- Stacey Abrams -

POLITICAL DISCOURSE

For several decades, disabled people have been spoken about with a particular lexicon. French politicians, relayed by media, talk about 'solidarity', 'courage', 'overcoming disability' and notably use, way too often, the following expression when talking about people with disabilities:

This expression calls to mind: Why was this perception established? How does it have to change? Indeed, this derogatory view towards disabled people shouldn't exist anymore, but, oddly, no accountability seems to be taken by the same people and institutions who implemented this cliché of the sad, bitter disabled person 'sustained by the government'.

The problem with this language, between emotion and condescension, is its faculty to put aside the most important: respect towards disabled people and their rights. This lack of interest reveals the difficulty and the unease to grasp a subject that concerns 12 million people in France (1).

In actuality, this number should be higher because many people don't know that their chronic pain and conditions are, in fact, disabilities but also because, often, they don't want to be considered as disabled given the implications (i.e prejudice).

During the 2017 International Day of People with Disabilities, Sophie Cluzel, the State Secretary in charge of disabled people, shares that 'one of the first things to do to achieve the inclusive society we all wish for is to change the perception towards difference (2).' Given that society is still not inclusive, it doesn't seem too risky to say... that this is not the case.

On the contrary, it's the government's role to set up inclusive policies to make sure that each citizen has the same rights, disabled or not. When laws make society truly inclusive with disabled people fully part of it, then this infamous 'perception change' can happen.

Furthermore, when in November 2018, the State Secretary was asked what actions the government is doing to fight ableism, her response was: 'It's a word that I don't know and that, in my opinion, is groundless. We have to stop pitting able-bodied and disabled people against each other. It just crystallizes dysfunctions. Disabled people's wish is to have the most ordinary life possible. We have to think in terms of universal conception for everybody to have a place without opposing interests (3).'

By responding that this expression is 'unfounded', the Secretary of State is denying an oppression she's supposed to be tackling and wants to discredit the fight of disabled activists. In addition, highlighting the fact that the term would oppose able-bodied and disabled people is particularly pernicious given that society's structure and policies from various governments have always separated disabled people from able-bodied people.

The discriminatory experiences shared by people with disabilities reflect a societal problem, an oppression lived in a collective manner. When laws and international conventions are not respected and dictate which spaces are accessible to disabled people or not, it is clearly the State that opposes both sides by separating and thus excluding disabled people from able-bodied people.

And identifying, naming, explaining, analyzing these discriminations is then necessary to put an end to the segregation that disabled people endure. Respecting disabled people's rights is not aiming to oppose anyone but, on the contrary, to include everybody.

The political discourse constructed upon a vague and emotional lexicon allows the government to distance itself from it and present disabled people's rights as a charity and not political. That's why, when governments establish policies in favor of people with disabilities' rights, words like 'effort' or 'gesture'(4) come up...

... And that a sort of acknowledgment and deference is expected from disabled people when, in reality, those are just 'reparations' of inequality, an inequality based on an arbitrary vision of who has the right to what.

How politicians see themselves when they put into place a law that benefits disabled people even though we are in the 21st century and it was about time:

A reminder: France actually ratified the 2010 United Nations International Convention related to people with disabilities' rights, where it recognizes disabled people's right 'to live in society with the same liberty of choice than other people'.

Consequently, we have governments that will talk the talk with language's elements repeated ad nauseum, like 'universal accessibility', but are not walking the walk as they actually are setting back disabled people's rights and autonomy (i.e. maintaining institutionalization, housing made less and less accessible, welfare being reduced and more monitored, etc.).

In parallel, every year in France, 2-3 public relations (PR) initiatives focus on disabled people:

• Politicians' 'role playing', which are 'non-actions that allow politicians to maintain a status quo and give them benefits in terms of image and likability (5)' according to Elena Chamorro, a disabled professor and co-founder of the French collective CLHEE (Collectif Lutte et Handicaps pour l'Egalité et l'Emancipation or Struggle and Disabilities Collective - For Equality and Emancipation).

She's exactly right.

• One-time events centered on work like the 'DuoDay', whose concept is the following: 'A company, a community or an organization welcomes a person with disabilities for a day to form a pair with a professional volunteer (6)'.

You will note that the word 'professional' only applies to the able-bodied person.

When we look closely, we can quickly figure out that what's important is not the fate of disabled people, who are patronized and objectified. Apparently, they don't have surnames and are often qualified as 'partners'.

Frédérique Vidal @VidalFrederique

A week ago, I had the pleasure to share my day with Marie, a young graduate from @EMNormandie during the #DuoDay2019. Let's go back to that day, which objective is to get things moving and change the perception of disability. (7)

Such an original tweet from the Minister of Education, Research and Innovation with this 'change of perception on disability'!

Moreover, finding a job doesn't really lead to anything if disabled people don't have the financial and human resources to go back-and-forth from work to home and if companies don't offer them a fully accessible work environment.

Nowadays, the exclusion of a certain part of the population from public space contributes to the complexities and added layers of the issues disabled people experience. And this results in able-bodied people being unaware of and not realizing the multitude of obstacles disabled people face daily. Moreover, the non-representation and non-implication of people with disabilities when these topics are discussed lead to either a policies' status quo or, even worse, a situation where rights are actually going backwards (like housing accessibility) with little accountability.

Therefore, it's essential to stop with these counterproductive elements of language and to focus policies and discourse related to disabled people around the respect of their rights, in direct collaboration with them.

If we want to push the thinking even further, we have to realize that a certain number of people with disabilities will never be included in the capitalist system we live in and its' outrageous performance goal and ask ourselves the following questions: which space is given to people that, given their limitations, can't work or work as much as other people? If a person has little to no production value, does this person still have a right to live a dignified life?

What is expected from truly progressive politicians is to remove barriers for disabled people to not be excluded from society due to their disability and to tackle structural violence so that they can lead autonomous lives and have access to the same opportunities.

“NOTHING ABOUT US WITHOUT US!”

Phrase coined by disabled South Africans and that symbolizes the fact that disabled people know what their needs are and, therefore, must fully participate in every discussions about them.

DEMANDS

As disability has always been treated as a charity issue and not as a civil rights one, this significantly impacts behaviors and policies regarding the inclusion of disabled people in society.

Consequently, the very idea that people with disabilities don't want to accept crumbs anymore but demand that their legitimate rights be respected challenges the patronizing treatment usually used towards them.

Also, French disability rights advocates have stopped relying on organizations who are also in charge of residential care facilities and specialized services in France, which are supposed to represent disabled people but actually agree with an ableist outlook on society and receive subsidies from the government to operate. Therefore, they cannot truly oppose power.

Summary of the current reality in France regarding disability, which concerns around 20% of the population:

- disability is the first cause for discrimination (1),
- very low accessibility from public space to housing,
- an institutionalization that segregates disabled people and forbids them to be fully free and autonomous,
- disabled people majorly face poverty and dependence due to a benefit - Allocation pour Adulte Handicapé or AAH - which is below the poverty line and is also calculated by taking into account the partner's salary,
- the extra charges related to disability - from mobility aids to treatments - are major ones,
- disabled people face enormous difficulties accessing education and employment,
- people with disabilities are constantly an afterthought, including in social movements and gatherings,
- in 2018, disabled people's media representation was only of 0.7% (2).

... Simply put: disabled people are excluded everywhere, all the time; a treatment that has been criticized by Catalina Devandas-Aguilar, the United Nations' Special Rapporteur on the Rights of Persons with Disabilities (3). And the ableist policies, that don't allow disabled people to get the necessary help to become as autonomous as possible, forces them to be even more dependant on other people, and notably their families, who are not paid for that job.

As the lack of accessibility excludes disabled people from numerous activists organizations and groups, Internet and social media offer opportunities for them to discover endless resources regarding the struggle for disabled people's rights but also to express themselves, appropriate a space, support one another and emancipate themselves.

Indeed, when activism cannot be 'physical', those platforms give another way to organize and let people with disabilities use their voices through tweets, videos, blogs, podcasts, memes... These types of content - like the following hashtags - inform, explain and allow to grasp the universality of disabled people's experiences in their daily lives.

#DisabledAndCute // Keah Brown

Encourages disabled people to take selfies and accept themselves.

#AbledsAreWeirds // Imani Barbarin

Recounts uncomfortable interactions with able-bodied people.

#InaccessibilityMeans // Emily Ladau

Shows the consequences of an inaccessible society.

#CripTheVote // Alice Wong, Gregg Beratan et Andrew Pulrang

Started during the 2016 US elections to point out disabled people's demands.

However, when disabled people share their experiences of discrimination, their words are often instantly discredited because, apparently, they 'make themselves look like a victim', an argument that is frequent when marginalized communities express themselves.

It would be great to have a more accessible society where everybody can easily move around and navigate!

You already have accessible buses, priority lines and parking spaces so you should be fine.

This habit to want to belittle and silence those who take the floor, an already grueling act, is very telling because being a victim of discrimination isn't a feeling but a fact.

Being treated differently is humiliating and noting a reality aiming for a real change to happen isn't 'victimizing' oneself.

... And that's what I call:

THE DISABILITY PARADOX

Disabled people are always celebrated as inspirations but aren't entitled to the same rights as able-bodied people.

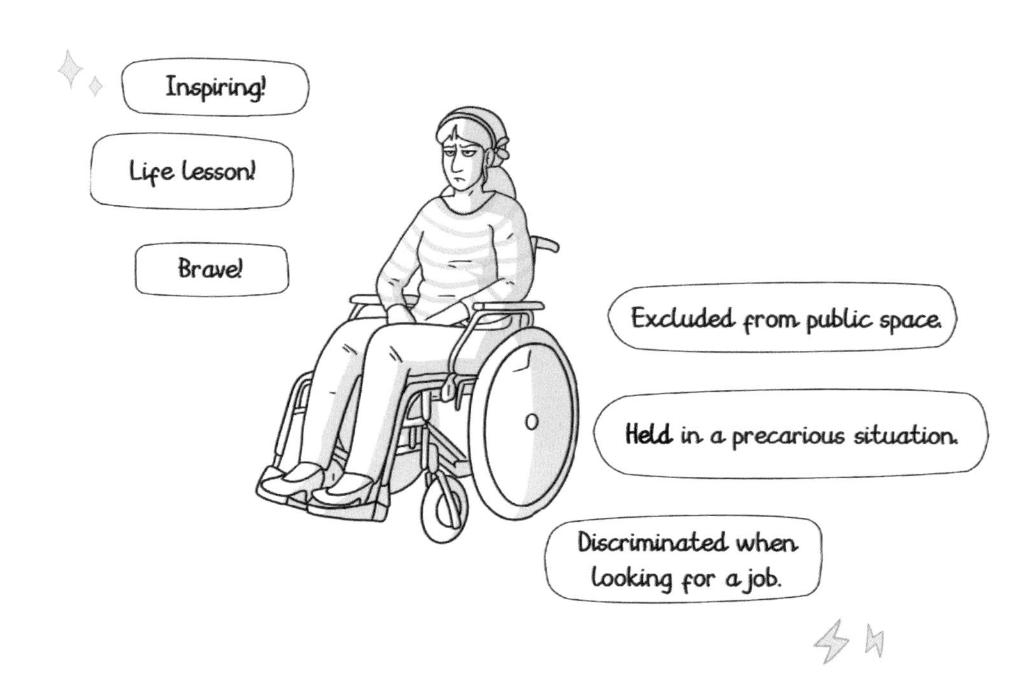

... which remains consistent in a ableist society where disabled people exist as objects and are not perceived as human beings.

INCLUSIVE FEMINISM

In France, within feminist movements, disabled women are also ignored and their demands are not considered even when:

- disabled women face huge difficulties regarding access to health, education, employment etc,
- 61% of those women have been victims of sexual harassment versus 54% of able-bodied women (4),
- women with disabilities, along with women of color, are more exposed to hostile behavior in the workplace (5).

Since #MeToo, disabled women have not been listened to even though they represent a large number of sexual assault victims.

'Some feminists fail to realize that we live in bodies. And therefore, we should highlight the fight against fatphobia and ableism as much as the fights for reproductive rights, equal salaries (6).'

Roxane Gay, American professor and editor.

It's also important to take into account the intersection of oppressions lived by disabled women, who endure at least sexism and ableism but who can also be subjected to racism, transphobia, Islamophobia and other oppressions.

Therefore, it is vital to listen to, read and let disabled women take the floor in the feminist movement so that it can include every woman.

Being vocal and active addressing ableism on the Internet, particularly as a woman, can quickly become exhausting. First, having to explain to someone that your existence deserves the same treatment as others is extremely brutal. On top of this, social media is filled with people who think they know issues related to someone's disability better than the person themselves...

An example, after having written several tweets regarding the Parisian subway lack of accessibility:

@

There are buses and tramways in Paris too, you know...

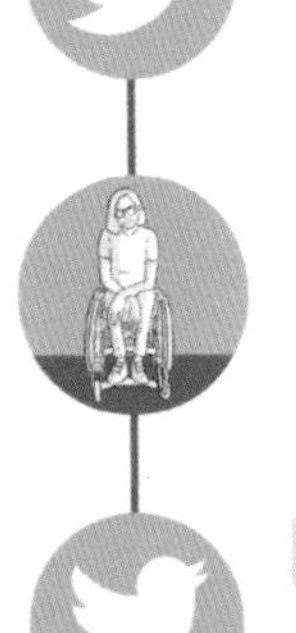

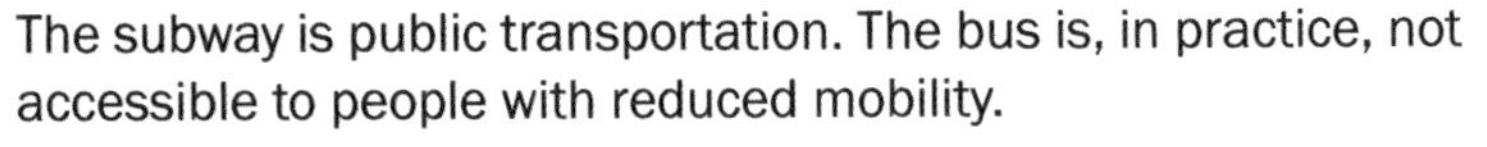

Marina Carlos @MarinaCpom

The subway is public transportation. The bus is, in practice, not accessible to people with reduced mobility.

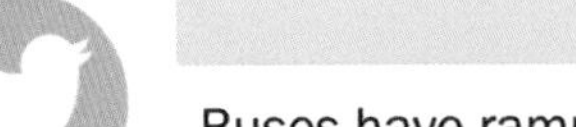

@

Buses have ramps and spaces reserved for disabled people.
I think you don't know anything about this subject.

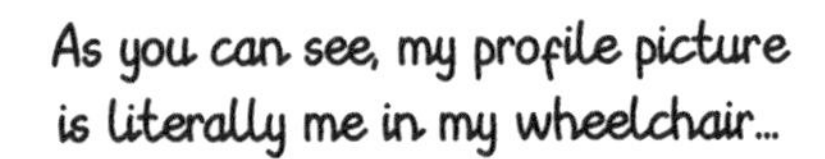

As you can see, my profile picture is literally me in my wheelchair...

To reclaim their place in a society that has always marginalized disabled people as well as claim they are people with rights shouldn't be a radical position but it still is today...

And tomorrow, I hope disabled people:

- will be treated with respect and have access to the same opportunities,
- will be at the center of all the discussions about them,
- will be represented in the media not because they are disabled but because they exist,
- will have the right to be spontaneous instead of having to spend a large amount of energy to organize every time they want to go out,
- won't have to adjust themselves to be accepted and included,
- and won't have the feeling of not being enough or, on the contrary, being too much.

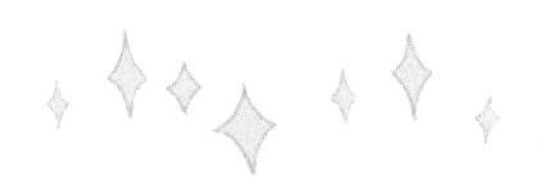

BONUS

ACTIVISTS TO FOLLOW

Social media allowed me to discover disabled activists, mostly English-speaking ones, who, through their content, made me feel understood, included, supported and helped me become aware of my voice and its' legitimacy.

ELISA ROJAS

Lawyer and co-founder of the CLHEE (Collectif Lutte et Handicaps pour l'Egalité et l'Emancipation or Struggle and Disabilities Collective - For Equality and Emancipation), Elisa Rojas actively campaigns against ableism and notably institutionalization. Very active on Twitter, she also writes texts on her blog 'Aux marches du palais' ('At the Palace's steps').

@elisarojasm

ANNIE SEGARRA

Annie Segarra is a queer, disabled, Latinx YouTuber and activist. She created the #TheFutureIsAccessible and her varied content talks, among others, about chronic illness, body image and mental health.

@annieelainey

IMANI BARBARIN

Communications director in Philadelphia, Imani Barbarin tweets and writes on her blog 'Crutches and Spice' her experiences as a disabled black woman. She started numerous viral hashtags like #ThingsDisabledPeopleKnow.

 @Imani_Barbarin

ALICE WONG

Alice Wong is the creator of Disability Visibility Project, an online community dedicated to creating, sharing and amplifying disability media and culture.
In 2015, she was the first person to visit the White House and meet the President of the United States, Barack Obama, through a robot.

 @SFdirewolf

ZIPPORAH ARIELLE

Zipporah Arielle writes and tweets about disabled people's rights, her bi identity, her Service-Dog-In-Training and her experience living in a jewish, queer, disabled body.

 @coffeespoonie

KEAH BROWN

Keah Brown is an American author and journalist (Teen Vogue, Marie Claire UK, Harper's Bazaar...). She created the viral #DisabledAndCute and her collection of essays, 'The Pretty One', came out in August 2019.

 @Keah_Maria

MARYANGEL GARCÍA-RAMOS

Maryangel García-Ramos is a Mexican activist, speaker and strategist who fights for disabled people's rights and created the 'Mexican women with disabilities' movement so that they can have access to the same opportunities.

MATTHIEU

Following his diagnosis, Matthieu decided to open a blog plus a YouTube channel named 'Vivre Avec' ('To Live With') to share and inform about his daily life with the Ehlers Danlos Syndrome. He is also very active on Twitter and Instagram, often seen with his 2 rabbits.

Dear familia, friends and notably Clémence, Johanna, Klervi & Imani: thank you from the bottom of my heart for your continuous love and support. I wouldn't be here without you.

And a huge thanks to Freaks for her creativity and enthusiasm regarding this project. It was a joy working with you!

MARINA CARLOS

Marina is a 31 years-old French-Portuguese born and raised in Paris who watches way too many TV Shows. After working during 5 years in the Social Media field, she now focuses on advocating for disabled people's rights. She writes mostly French and English content about ableism and notably regarding accessibility as well as media representation of people with disabilities. *I'll figure it out: How ableism impacts disabled people's lives* is her first book.

marinacarlos.com
instagram.com/marinacpom
twitter.com/marinacpom

FREAKS

Self-taught artist-author, Freaks has been writing, illustrating and publishing graphic novels for more than 5 years. Although being specialized in animal art, she diversifies her work in her publications: *Punk* (2015), *Rose* (2017), *Je ne serai pas ta muse* (2019), as well as this book. Very active in the punk environment, her activism within anti-ableism and body positive movements has a direct impact on her work.

freaks-illustrations.fr/
instagram.com/freaksdessin
twitter.com/freaks_dessin

SITOGRAPHY

ABLEISM

1. The Disability Price Tag 2019 Policy report by Scope
https://tinyurl.com/ycy6alfv
2. The #MeToo Movement Has Ignored Disabled People, But We Need It More Than Ever by D'Arcee Neal - April 16, 2018
https://tinyurl.com/y7zt2ysb
3. Forced Intimacy: An Ableist Norm by Mia Mingus - August 6, 2017
http://tinyurl.com/ybpo726s
4. Tweets by @twitchyspoonie - January 4, 2019
https://tinyurl.com/yao2lwy6 // https://tinyurl.com/yc4jk96q

ACCESSIBILITY

1. Access denied: wheelchair metro maps versus everyone else's by Nick Van Mead, Harvey Symons and Aghnia Adzkia - September 21, 2017
https://tinyurl.com/ycrbwfqk
2. À Byis, le métro passe au bleu by Émilie Defay - December 11, 2018
https://tinyurl.com/y7eyjye8
3. City Buses Are Wheelchair-Accessible, But Disabled Riders Still Face Obstacles by Jeanmarie Evelly - July 2, 2018
https://tinyurl.com/y9yj6y2q
4. Why London's subway system leaves so many disabled people without a ride by Noah Richardson - September 3, 2018
https://tinyurl.com/y8crftnp
5. Accessibilité PSH
https://tinyurl.com/y85wy738
6. Air Travel Consumer Report - February 2019
https://tinyurl.com/y9mhprza
7. Tweet de @mssinenomine - May 15, 2019
https://tinyurl.com/y7cb53m4
8. Interview with Pierre Dufour - December 2018

MEDIA REPRESENTATION

1. À 16 ans, elle danse malgré le handicap by Brut - January 14, 2019
https://tinyurl.com/yckbbzuq
2. RJ Mitte : l'acteur de Breaking Bad devient mannequin malgré son handicap by Clara Crochemore - July 28, 2015
http://tinyurl.com/yaceaj8n

3. Marseille : quand la passion dépasse le handicap by Yves Torino - February 5, 2019
http://tinyurl.com/y7hgms33
4. The Cost of Being Disabled by Imani Barbarin - May 2019
https://tinyurl.com/y9zymg6o
5. Cutting disability services doesn't save money. But it does damage lives by Frances Ryan - April 4, 2019
https://tinyurl.com/y6yhsufg
6. Selma Blair Became A Disabled Icon Overnight. Here's Why We Need More Stories Like Hers by Zipporah Arielle - March 6, 2019
https://tinyurl.com/yyoua9of
7. I'm not your inspiration, thank you very much by Stella Young - April 2014
https://tinyurl.com/y7htkj6u
8. Ilnequality in 1,100 Popular Films: Examining Portrayals of Gender, Race/Ethnicity, LGBT & Disability from 2007 to 2017 by Dr. Stacy L. Smith, Marc Choueiti, Dr. Katherine Pieper - July 2018
https://tinyurl.com/y7lmvjmy
9. Able-Bodied Actors Play 95% of Disabled Characters in Top 10 TV Shows, Says New Study by Elizabeth Wagmeister - July 13, 2016
https://tinyurl.com/y82hdrys
10. Maysoon Zayid: "We are not making history, we are changing the story" by Xiaorong Chen
https://tinyurl.com/yb679f88
11. Test de Bechdel
https://tinyurl.com/pumlvrt
12. The Kent Test created by Clarkisha Kent
https://tinyurl.com/yb9g56zv
13. Sinéad Burke On Becoming The First Little Person To Attend The Met Gala by Sinéad Burke - May 7, 2019
https://tinyurl.com/yc7zqty3

POLITICAL DISCOURSE

1. Enquête HID de l'INSEE de 2001
2. Tweet de @s_cluzel - December 4, 2017
http://tinyurl.com/ydyy98r5
3. Sophie Cluzel : « Ce n'est pas aux personnes handicapées de s'adapter systématiquement, mais à l'entreprise » by Sylvie Laidet - November 18, 2018
https://tinyurl.com/ycqyxl4w
4. Logements accessibles aux handicapés : le gouvernement fait un geste by Isabelle Rey-Lefebvre - September 26, 2018
https://tinyurl.com/yd86xtkk

5. Dépolitisation et regard valido-centré : les mises en situation by Elena Chamorro - May 28, 2019
https://tinyurl.com/y9oldkav
6. DuoDay, on vous explique tout !
http://tinyurl.com/ycd682vo
7. Tweet by @VidalFrederique - May 24, 2019
http://tinyurl.com/ycccnozr

DEMANDS

1. Rapport annuel d'activité 2018
https://tinyurl.com/y7kerqgz
2. Baromètre de la diversité 2018 - Représentation de la diversité à la télévision : des progrès restent à faire - January 16, 2019
https://tinyurl.com/ydcvdk7x
3. Version EasyRead du rapport sur les droits des personnes handicapées de la Rapporteuse spéciale lors de sa visite en France (A/HRC/40/54/Add.1)
https://tinyurl.com/ydcdoykd
4. Enquête « Violences à l'égard des femmes » de l'Agence des droits fondamentaux de l'Union européenne de mars 2016
5. Baromètre 2018 de la perception des discriminations dans l'emploi - Défenseur des droits et l'Organisation internationale du travail
https://tinyurl.com/y9vonrew
6. Roxane Gay : « La grossophobie dans les espaces queer est bien plus douloureuse et frustrante » by Olga Volfson - January 18, 2019
https://tinyurl.com/ybk857pk

Printed in Great Britain
by Amazon